W9-AAF-162

CREATIVITY
JOURNAL
FOR KIDS

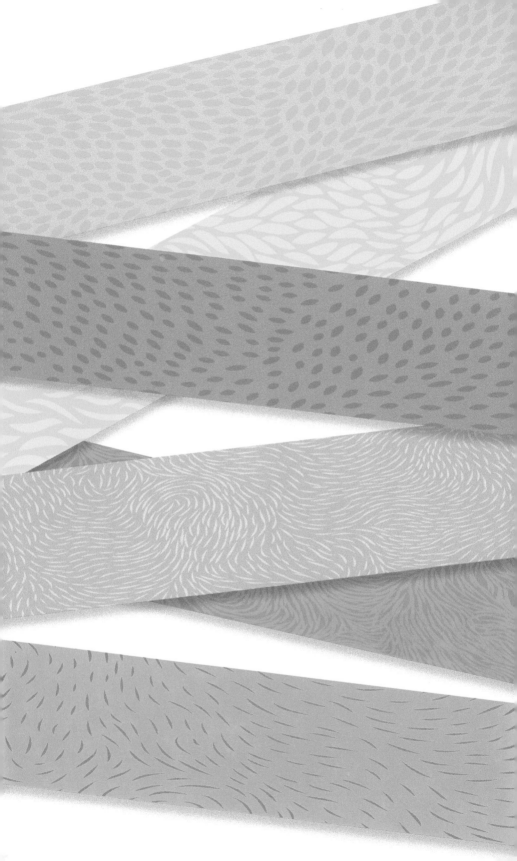

CREATIVITY
JOURNAL
for Kids

Fun Activities to Spark Imagination and Inspire Self-Expression

Clara Deneen
Valerie Deneen

ROCKRIDGE
PRESS

Copyright © 2021 by Rockridge Press, Emeryville, California

No part of this publication may be reproduced, stored in a retrieval system, or transmitted in any form or by any means, electronic, mechanical, photocopying, recording, scanning, or otherwise, except as permitted under Sections 107 or 108 of the 1976 United States Copyright Act, without the prior written permission of the Publisher. Requests to the Publisher for permission should be addressed to the Permissions Department, Rockridge Press, 6005 Shellmound Street, Suite 175, Emeryville, CA 94608.

Limit of Liability/Disclaimer of Warranty: The Publisher and the author make no representations or warranties with respect to the accuracy or completeness of the contents of this work and specifically disclaim all warranties, including without limitation warranties of fitness for a particular purpose. No warranty may be created or extended by sales or promotional materials. The advice and strategies contained herein may not be suitable for every situation. This work is sold with the understanding that the Publisher is not engaged in rendering medical, legal, or other professional advice or services. If professional assistance is required, the services of a competent professional person should be sought. Neither the Publisher nor the author shall be liable for damages arising herefrom. The fact that an individual, organization, or website is referred to in this work as a citation and/or potential source of further information does not mean that the author or the Publisher endorses the information the individual, organization, or website may provide or recommendations they/it may make. Further, readers should be aware that websites listed in this work may have changed or disappeared between when this work was written and when it is read.

For general information on our other products and services or to obtain technical support, please contact our Customer Care Department within the United States at (866) 744-2665, or outside the United States at (510) 253-0500.

Rockridge Press publishes its books in a variety of electronic and print formats. Some content that appears in print may not be available in electronic books, and vice versa.

TRADEMARKS: Rockridge Press and the Rockridge Press logo are trademarks or registered trademarks of Callisto Media Inc. and/or its affiliates, in the United States and other countries, and may not be used without written permission. All other trademarks are the property of their respective owners. Rockridge Press is not associated with any product or vendor mentioned in this book.

Interior and Cover Designer: Jami Spittler
Art Producer: Sara Feinstein
Editor: Nicky Montalvo
Production Editor: Ruth Sakata Corley
Production Manager: Michael Kay

Illustrations © 2021 Risa Culbertson, p. 11, 13, 14-15, 26-27, 30-31, 40-41, 44-45, 50-51, 54-55, 58-59, 62-63, 66-67, 70-71, 76, 78-79, 82-83, 88-89, 94, 96-97, 103, 105, 108-109, 112-113, 116-117, 120, 124-126, 132-134, 142. All other art used under license from Shutterstock.com and iStock.com.

ISBN: Print 978-1-64876-993-1| eBook 978-1-64876-994-8

R0

This book
belongs to:

WELCOME!

Get ready to unleash the creativity creature inside you. Sometimes, that creativity creature may be daring. Other times, it may be silly or serious, or even a little destructive. It's up to you—in this book, anything goes. If you ever need a break from school or chores, or even if you're just sitting around, open this book and explore. You'll find many ways to be creative, have fun, and use your imagination. Enjoy and go wild!

INSTRUCTIONS:

 There are no rules. The activities in this book are only suggestions, so you can do them in any way you choose.

There is no order. Feel free to skip around.

3 You don't need to complete every activity. Do whatever you like.

4 There is no right or wrong way to complete this book. Creativity can be expressed in many ways, and this book should never hold you back.

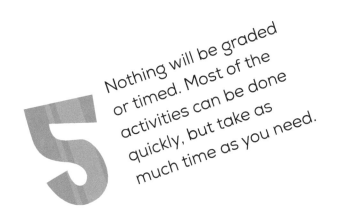

5 Nothing will be graded or timed. Most of the activities can be done quickly, but take as much time as you need.

complimentary
BOOKMARKS

Use these pages to write nice things about yourself.
Rip them out. Fold them. Use them as bookmarks.

Well, That's Ah-peel-ing!

After eating a piece of your favorite fruit, dry the peels and tape them to these pages.

SPIN INTO ACTION!

Use a paper clip and a pencil as a spinner. Write actions (like "jump") in the left spinner spaces.

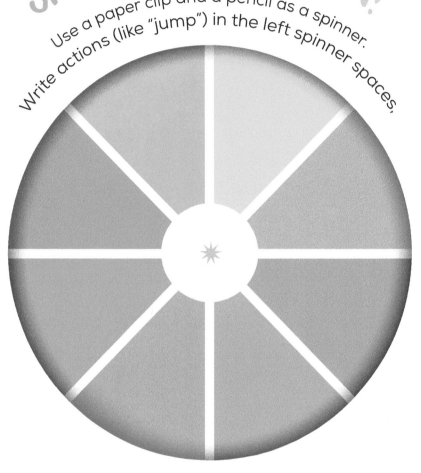

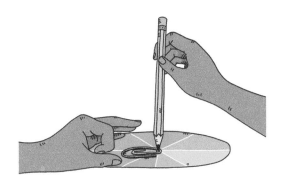

and write adverbs (words that end in -ly, like "slowly") in the right spinner. Spin, and do whatever the spaces say.

Pretend Pet

Pretend this book is your pet. Tie a string to it. Take it for a walk. Talk to it if you wish.

SEIZE THE (HOLI)DAY!

Invent an exciting NEW holiday with its own traditions. Convince your family and friends to join in the celebration. Tape photos or mementos of the festivities to these pages.

I HEREBY DECLARE THAT THE

_____ DAY OF THE MONTH OF

_____

SHALL FOREVER BE KNOWN AS

_____

FROM THIS DAY FORWARD.

PHOTOS & MEMENTOS HERE

Make
Some ~~Noise~~ Music!

How many ways can
you find to make music
with this book?

Tell a story on this page

and then hide it inside a library book.

Fill out this page and then hide it for a friend to find.

POSTCARD

TO:

FROM:

IK 15

NO HATS

Use chalk to declare a "no-hat zone" on a sidewalk or driveway. Proudly wear this book as a hat in the no-hat zone.

ALLOWED

POCKET-SIZE PRESENTS

Use these pages to create gift tags and distribute small gifts to people.

YOU'VE GOT THE BEAT!

Find 2 sticks and use this page as a drum pad. How many different rhythms can you make?

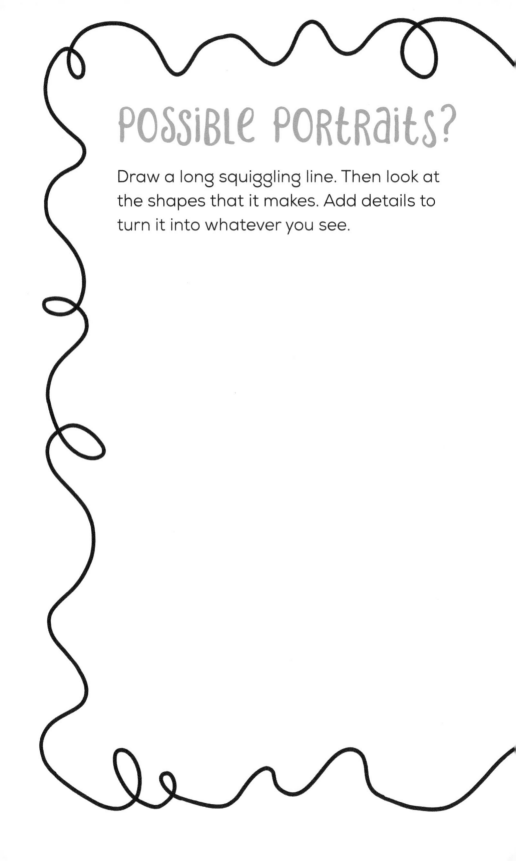

POSSIBLE PORTRAITS?

Draw a long squiggling line. Then look at
the shapes that it makes. Add details to
turn it into whatever you see.

Lovely Labels

Create a collage using labels or packaging from things you've eaten.

Collect seeds or crumbs from food you have eaten and tape them onto these pages.

SAVIN' IT FOR LATER

TODAY'S MENU:

WISHING WALL

Write a wish on one of the bricks. Pass these pages around to your family or friends so they can add a wish, too.

CARTOON CAPTIONS

Outdoor Color Match

Punch a hole in each color swatch. Go outside and try to match up the colors with things in your neighborhood. Write about all the matches you find.

Place this book facedown on these pages. Slide it across the floor to a friend.

Smooth

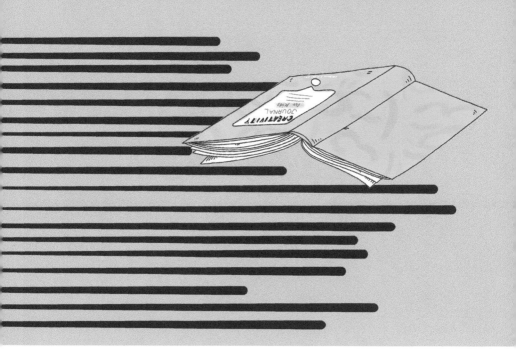

Sliding

Have them
slide it back.
Repeat
as desired.

BULL'S-EYE!

Rip out this page. Ball it up. Use the next page for target practice.

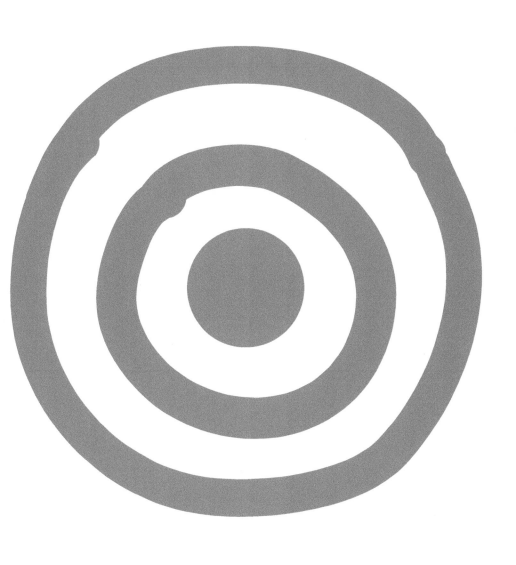

FUTURE MAIL

Imagine yourself in the future. Write a letter to your current self all about the wonderful things you've

done and the goals you've achieved.

Scratch-N-Sniff

Add 2 tablespoons of water to a packet of unsweetened powdered drink mix. Paint with the mixture on these pages to create a scratch-and-sniff masterpiece.

SEASONAL SKETCHES

WINTER

SPRING

Draw a tree for every season. Pick your favorite drawing.

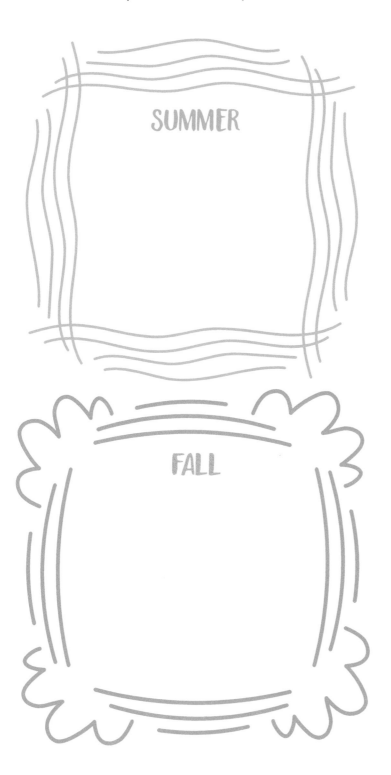

SUMMER

FALL

HAY! HORSES ARE HARD TO DRAW!

Horses are especially difficult to draw.
Draw at least one from memory here.
Don't erase anything!

EGG-CELLENT USES

1   2   3

7   8   9

Write down as many uses as you can think of for an egg carton.

SLAMMIN' PRINTS

Find colorful flowers or fallen leaves outside. Place them on these pages and cover them with a paper towel. Smash them with a hammer.

INTERESTING
INVESTIGATION

Research something you think is boring.
What about it is actually fascinating?

Trash to Treasure

Make note of any litter you see outside. Think about and list all the ways the litter could be useful.

Nature Notes

Tape leaves and other objects found in nature to these pages.

HORRIFYING HUMOR

Write a joke about
something that scares you.

Mindful Moment

For one day, write or draw the first thing that comes to your mind every hour. Be honest and don't erase anything!

8:00 a.m.

9:00 a.m.

10:00 a.m.

11:00 a.m.

Noon

1:00 p.m.

2:00 p.m.

3:00 p.m.

4:00 p.m.

5:00 p.m.

6:00 p.m.

Feeling Pages

Draw or write on these pages when you are feeling sad or have other big feelings.

YOUR #1 FAN

Decorate the next page and fold it into a paper fan.

Secure the end with tape. Use it on a hot day.

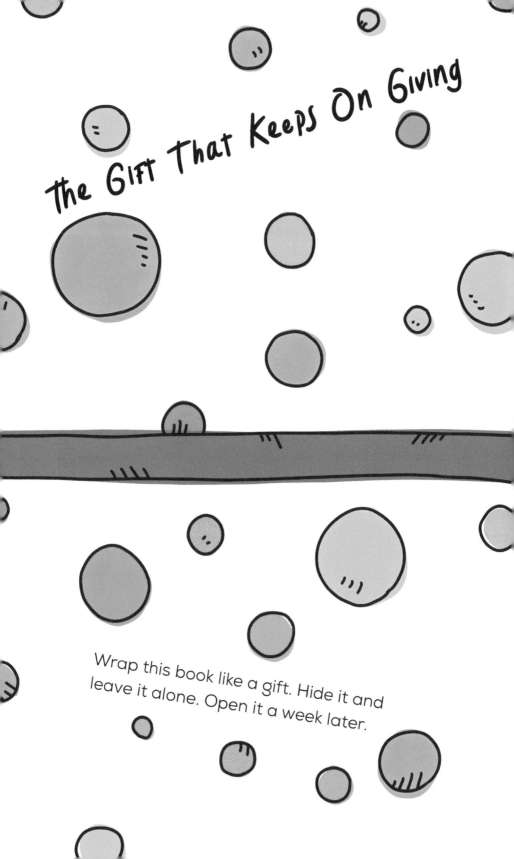

the Gift That Keeps On Giving

Wrap this book like a gift. Hide it and leave it alone. Open it a week later.

Illustrate some of your favorite jokes here. Share your artwork with someone who needs a good laugh.

Run around outside. Afterward, jump on these pages.

JUMP ON
THE JOURNAL

Paint on these pages while
listening to fancy classical music.

Classy Doodles

THIS IS FOR THE BIRDS!

Make a tray to feed the birds. Cut along the solid lines and fold on the dotted lines. Tape the corners together. Fill with birdseed or bread crumbs. Write about any wildlife that comes along.

STELLAR PLANETARIUM

Poke holes through the stars on these pages.
Shine a light through them.
Make your room a planetarium.

Balance this book on your finger. Try to spin it.

BALANCING BOOK

Have a Ball!

Tear this page into small pieces.
Ball them up and dip them into paint.
Allow them to dry.
Paste them back here.

REALLY GOOD
RECONSIDERATIONS

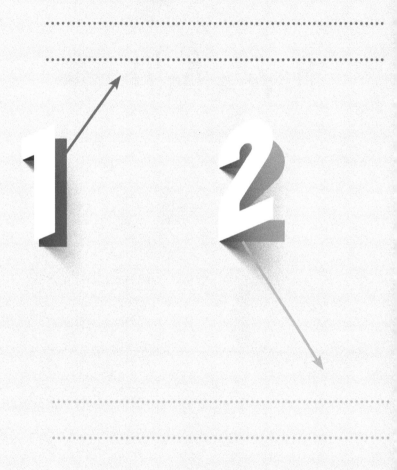

Think about something you strongly dislike.
List 5 things that aren't actually so bad about it.

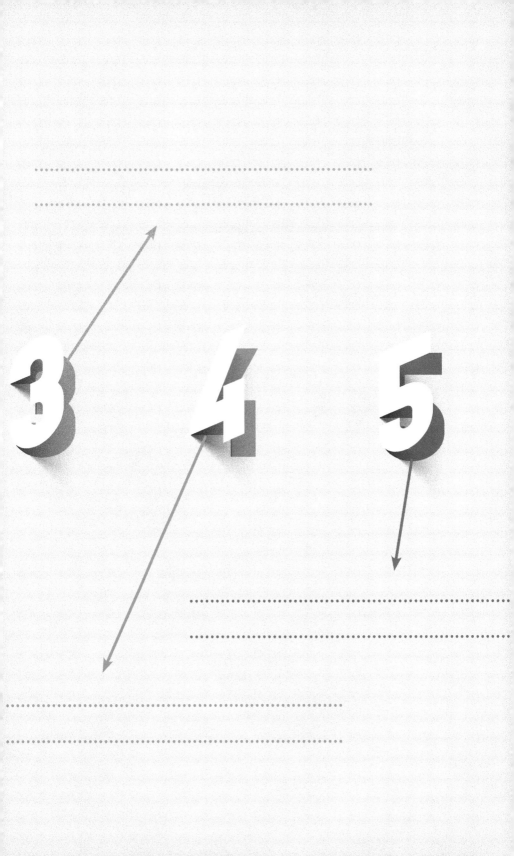

Good Catch!

catch it without dropping it.

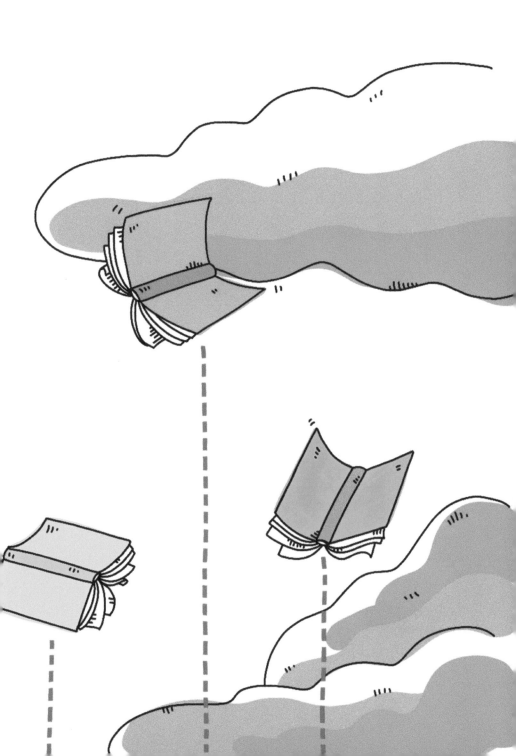

COMMUNITY COMPLIMENTS

Make a "take one compliment" sheet. Cut on the dotted lines, then write a compliment on each flap. Post it on a community bulletin board.

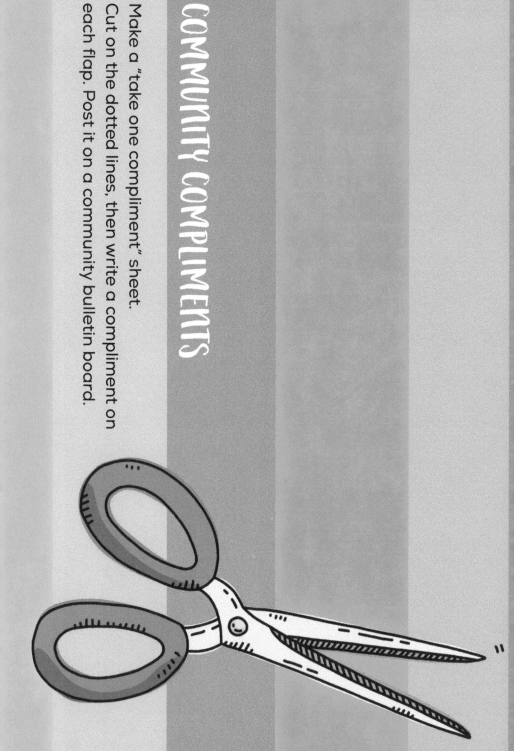

PLEASE TAKE ONE

SOLE SEARCHING

Using crayons, collect rubbings of shoe soles for every person in your household. Label and date them.

Surprise Drawing

Fold this page.
Create a hidden drawing inside the fold.

Veggie Verses

Write poems about your least favorite vegetables.

Sweet
Somethings

Think about a time someone
complimented you. Write about
it here. Then give a compliment
to someone else!

PENCIL PAGES

List as many uses as you can think of for a pencil.

Movin' and Groovin'

While walking around a room, hold a
pencil lightly on these pages. See what
marks it makes. Turn the squiggles into various objects.

BURST YOUR

THESE DOODLES ROCK!

Collect 5 rocks from outside.
Trace them on these pages.

Puffy Paint Pastries

Mix equal parts shaving cream and school glue with a few drops of poster paint. Add the mixture to a plastic zip-top bag. Cut off a bottom corner of the bag and squeeze the "icing" onto these pastries. Allow to dry, then feel its texture.

SUPERHERO
TRANSFORMATION

On the left page, list some things that make you different from everyone else. On the right page, draw a superhero version of yourself that uses these differences as strengths.

Collect small colorful objects from every room of your home. Glue or tape them to this page to create a collage.

STRONG SENTIMENTS

have but feel very strongly about.

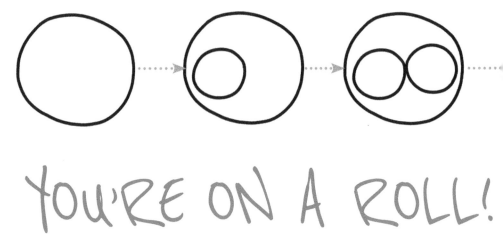

YOU'RE ON A ROLL!

Turn these circles into objects.

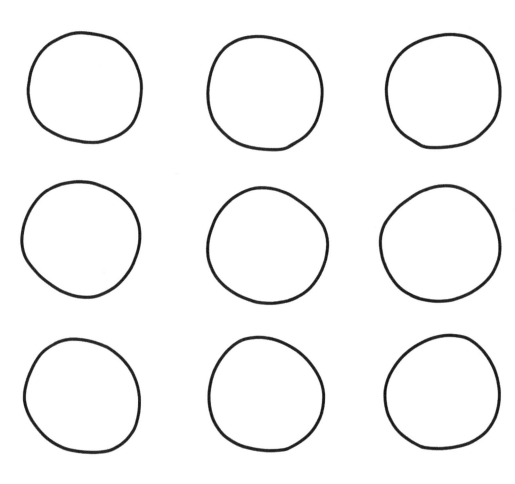

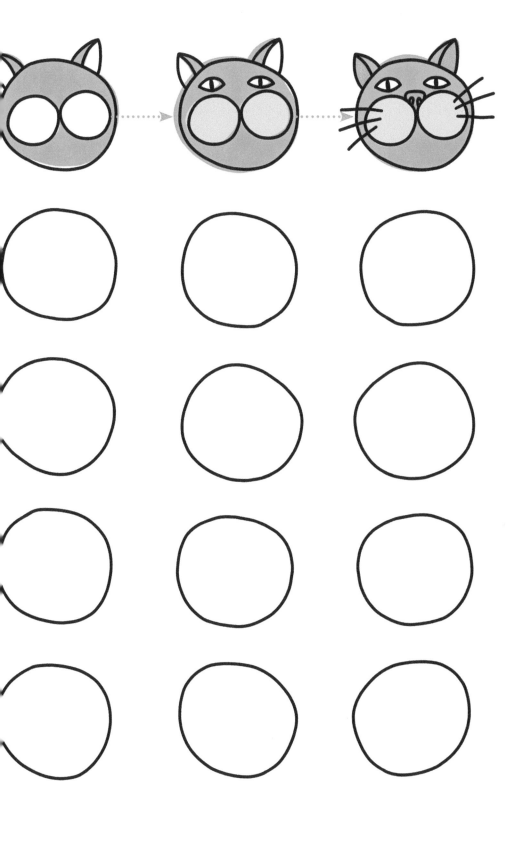

SURPRISE SYMMETRY

Paint on this page. While the paint is still wet, close the book. Open it back up. Once it dries, turn the painting into something new.

Assist List

List all the ways you
could help someone.

Use this page to collect 6 different textures (rough, fuzzy, smooth, sticky—whatever!). Have a friend close their eyes and try to identify them without looking.

TRiCKY TeXTURES

Season this soup by rubbing your favorite
fragrant herbs or seasonings into it.

Y'ALL BREADY FOR THIS?

NAME: _____

Ingredients: _____

_____

_____

_____

_____

_____

_____

_____

Create a new sandwich. Name it after yourself. Record the (soon-to-be) famous recipe here. Make and serve it to your friends or family to taste test.

Directions:

_____

_____

_____

_____

_____

_____

_____

_____

MORNING MUSINGS

Use these pages to write whatever pops into your head first thing in the morning. Write as fast as you can.

Coming Through!

Smear a bike or wheelchair wheel with dirt, finger paint, water, or coffee grounds, and then roll over this page.

PUDDLE

Rip out these pages. Drop them in a puddle. Jump on them

JUMP!

Pull them out. Let them dry. Put them back in the book.

A Clothes Encounter

Search the pockets of your dirty laundry.
Sketch or draw what you find. Look closely.

FANCY FOOTWEAR

For one day or even
a few hours, wear
2 different shoes. Did
anyone notice?

☐ YES

☐ NO

Was it a big deal?

....

....

....

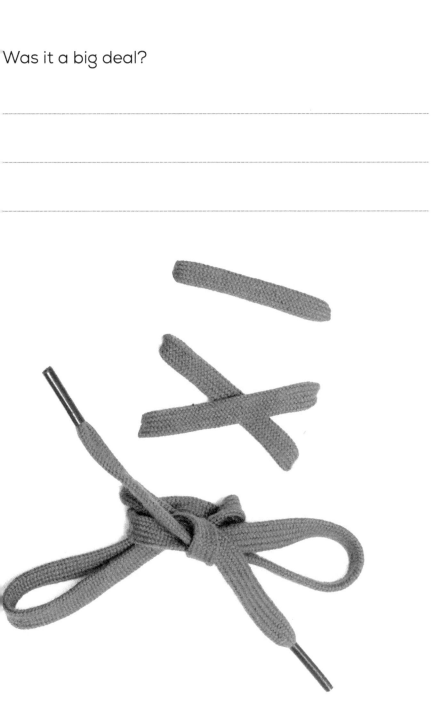

These Pages Might Come In Handy

Use these pages to wipe your hands after making some messy art.

Courageous Checklist

List some new things you could bravely try.
Think of foods, sports, languages, hobbies—anything!

- [ ] 1 ....
- [ ] 2 ....
- [ ] 3 ....
- [ ] 4 ....
- [ ] 5 ....
- [ ] 6 ....
- [ ] 7 ....
- [ ] 8 ....
- [ ] 9 ....
- [ ] 10 ....

MASQUERADE MAKER

Use the next page to make a funny mask.
Wear it around your home or in public.

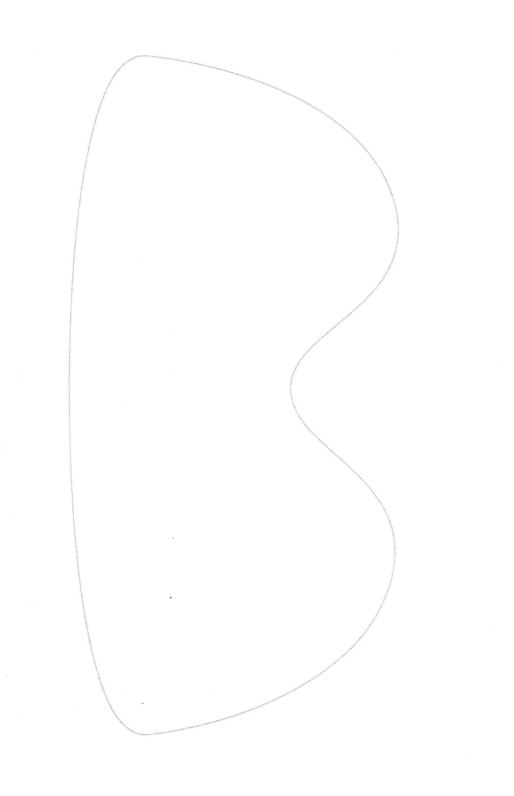

A Terrible Towel

After a shower, use this page
as a towel to dry your wet hair.

Happiness
Haiku

Write a poem
about something
that makes you happy.

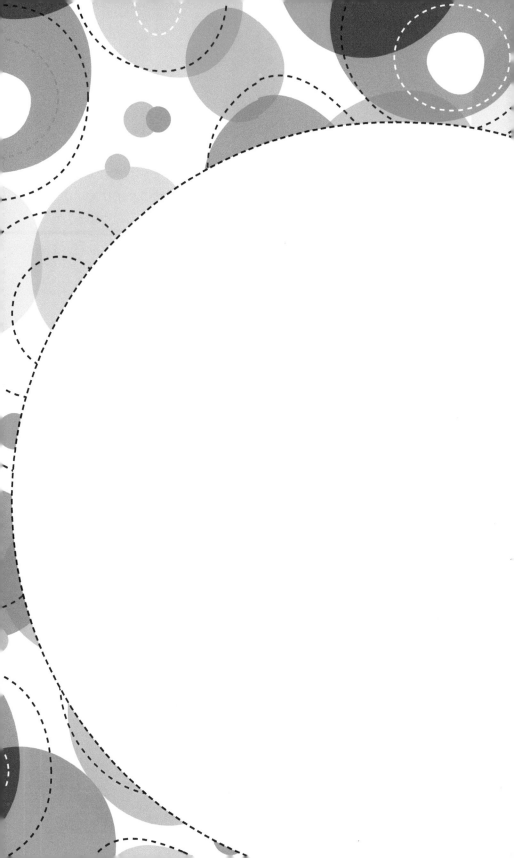

About the Authors

Valerie and **Clara Deneen** are a mother–daughter duo who value creativity and curiosity. Together, they share ideas for creative play, toy reviews, and activities on their website at InnerChildFun.com. Valerie is also the author of four books: *HORSES!*, *DOGS!*, *Cute Cats*, and *Cute Pets*, as well as the forthcoming book *Trucks, Cars, and Airplanes*. This is Clara's first book as a co-author, and she very much enjoys wearing hats in "no-hat zones."

CPSIA information can be obtained
at www.ICGtesting.com
Printed in the USA
JSHW031311240621
16197JS00004B/30